Radiant.

White.

Light.

radiant. white. light.

a divorce memoir in poems and stories

MO DUFFY

Pownal Street Press
CHARLOTTETOWN

"That First Christmas" first appeared in *The Globe and Mail,* Dec. 23, 2023.

www.moduffy.com

pownal street press

www.pownalstreetpress.com

Cataloging data available from Library and Archives Canada
ISBN 978-1-998129-73-7 · eBook ISBN 978-1-998129-74-4

Edited by Danielle Leowen · Copyedited by Alison Strumberger · Typeset by Jordan Beaulieu

Pownal Street Press gratefully acknowledges Mi'kma'ki, the ancestral and unceded territory of the Mi'kmaq First Nation on whose land our office is located.

Printed and bound in Canada by Friesens.

1 2 3 4 5 26 27 28 29 30

for the ones

who are exploding

TABLE OF CONTENTS

"Heartbreak doesn't break you, it breaks you open."

—*Jay Shetty*, 8 Rules of Love

for the record

Whatever this is, it is nothing.
It is everything, it is a tale of the
wild unfolding of a love, of a life, of a family.

As each layer peels, there are ten more behind it.
It is shock, wonder, trepidation, love, fear, and generosity of spirit.
It is shared experience, it is deep breaths.
It is historical.

It is a new beginning.

introduction

losing daydreams

The camp drop-off was a murder scene. I mean, it was Saturday, right? Or was it Sunday? I called ahead. It was Saturday. I texted, I emailed. I had to get the time right—was it 11:30 or was it 12? I'd better get there early. I'd better get there a day early, two days early. I'd better...

Goosy had gone through too much.

His dad and I were separating, but it was beautiful, and it was magical, because I knew there was someone out there who was better for my husband than me. And when his tears finally stopped, he said that it was true, and it was time for him to say it out loud—that if he was being honest, the partner who was best for him was not a woman, but a man.

So we held onto each other for dear life, like nothing would ever change, and we swayed in a gentle breeze until we couldn't hold on any longer, and we moved past shame and we moved past betrayal and into an empty space where neither of us knew who we belonged to anymore.

The camp for Goosy had been my idea. I just wanted him to do something different this summer, to expand his world view, to commune with nature. He needed the breath of new friendships, away from the entanglement of family changes that had characterized his Grade 5 year. And he'd have his cousins, and sports, and time to think.

It wasn't until I started packing for Ontario that I realized how disoriented I was from the move. My passport was somewhere in the mix. I began to hear the waterfall through the trees, water pounding against rocks.

I held back tears during the art camp drop-off with my youngest, Veda. My oldest, Leila, was going off to college, and I had to take her there, had to unpack her lipstick, the poetry books that she ordered online after she and Mister Lover Boy quit. For a high school crush, god, it was hard on all of us.

I had to admit, I was going through a lot.

I *wanted* love to work, I wanted it to. I didn't want to teach my daughter that even the strongest links can be broken. But still, the messaging was there: never lose what's yours, never take what's not given. Teaching her to lead with skepticism would go against the very operating system I'd put every effort to mother into her: *Lead with your heart.*

When I found my passport, I pushed my fingers slowly over my name on the signature page. In the last six months, everything in my life had changed. I was a different person.

The ponytail, though. I recognized her.

The eyes and the memory of when Passport Canada changed the rules. *Don't smile.* And for three times I tried not to smile, until I had sufficiently embarrassed the gangly teenager working at the Shoppers Drug Mart photo lab.

That girl existed. And behind her there were student IDs, old book reviews, printed-out columns from her very first published articles and even a memoir, and a hundred old friends and the people and the experiences that made her—old canoes and cottage parties and The Girl She Was Before—before she was married. And she was whole, and she was beautiful, and she was a complete person, and she needed no one, and she had a plan, and she had a dream, and she was prepared to do it alone—until a blond-haired man came along and distracted her with his surfing, and his road trips, and the look in his longing blue eyes, his duct taped wallets, and his playlists, and most of all, the way he let her take care of him.

And my god, I loved him.

The way he let me look at a map, and just say, *there*. The way he lined up dirt roads for us to drive down, and how we twirled in long grass and lupins and blew dandelions with toddlers, like time was a fiction, and we were suspended in a moment, intertwined in a dream, like it was real, like it was real. And he could see my vision and when he measured the angles, he could make it work. And he calculated, and he organized, and I dreamed it, and he built it. And for me, he stacked one dream upon the next, upon the next. Then a baby. Then a house. Then a master's. Then a business.

The way he told me that anything was possible. And for sixteen years, it *was.*

I rolled up jeans and t-shirts, scarves. *I should take my journal*, I thought. I'd been writing a mess of poems. But just like the passport before it—in a house just weeks old, its corners still teetering with boxes—the journal had not yet surfaced. I searched, deciphering my scribbled labels on the boxes, shoving my hands in randomly and feeling for it. That pink journal held my examination of divorce culture: poetry, essay, the past, the present. The bright lights, the takeaways, the guideposts. *Radiant. White. Light.*

I felt dizzy. What if it was gone? Passed away? The book itself, the dreams, the ideas? Like the marriage, it had dissolved into the ether. I checked the bookshelf, under the couch cushion. Still, *nothing.*

The journal held a rush of words. A time when we were easily lost, when we existed only for each other, in the middle of the night, in the dark, in windows, in refracted light on glass, in broken teacups. We were filled with time, filled with desire, filled with longing.

The past: a time when we were a box for each other, a vessel to be filled with certainty, with security, with the hopes of our parents and the dreams of our children. A time when I could only see him, and could only hear him, and he was my breath and I was his dreams. And we lived only for each other.

And I heard the waterfall again: solid to liquid, liquid to gas. I needed to focus now. We just had to get to camp. *Yes, to camp*. And suddenly everything I had was in a pile, and the waterfall was only the blood rushing in my ears.

The journal was gone.

The cover read, *daydreams*. If it wasn't here, where was it? Did I leave it at the beach, or in the cafe? I thought of Hemingway's suitcase, his hand scratched notes left under the seat of a train. Was my journal written only to be lost, was that the real poetry?

Maybe it was never meant to be read.

But what if someone *did* read it? The poem about that morning at breakfast, at the dance competition when I sat in a hotel lobby in a stiff chair, in godforsaken Fredericton or Moncton or wherever it was, that someone thought that cold butter on toast with a plastic knife passed for a decent breakfast, gave you sustenance, gave you life. And where you overheard the woman interrupt the man to ask him if she was his first wife or second? And for a moment I imagined there was a world where all of this was all over: a breath, a dream, a nightmare, just a sock lost in the wash, the end of a summer fling.

And I presumed that the breakup wasn't the crushing, deadly pain that made me physically ill, that caused me seizures and the jagged delirium after. And maybe in some lobby somewhere, someday, I too would talk recklessly about my life and my relationships, and someone may actually ask me, *Was that your first husband, or your second?* Like I might confuse the two. And I might throw my head back and laugh, and say, *Please save your questions to the end.*

The universe was signalling that the storm of the breakup was over. The process, however unbearable, had been now set adrift, circles of heat pushed off to the east, creating waves in the middle of the Atlantic; tropical storms moving somewhere else for a change.

I shook myself loose. *Goose needed his mom right now, and his whistle, and his seven pairs of shorts.*

By the time I was ready to go, I was dizzy and had to ask Mom to drive us since I really didn't feel well. And I wondered why I was doing this—*why did I always do this?*—over-plan and over-arrange and sign people up for things that they didn't want to do because they weren't me, and they didn't like camping, and they were actually fine to play video games all summer, and bike-gang around with the neighbourhood scraps.

But it was all too late now, and we were heading for Toronto. And I had a sinking feeling in my stomach, and his bag was so heavy he couldn't lift it, and my poems were in the wind, and my marriage was swirling in the atmosphere, and I would just have to make it all work. And when we boarded, I felt the rush of dopamine; we were doing it! We checked into the fanciest hotel in the city and took pictures of each other at the top of the CN Tower and made peace signs beside the aquarium's biggest brightest jellyfish, that just floated through space, and I wondered what kind of lessons it could teach me, to be, *to just be.*

We arrived at the rink with the world's largest pack and waited for the bus to Algonquin. And we watched the grass grow, and a baseball tournament for a while, and Goose entertained himself. But the time grew long, and the sun went high in the sky, and I knew that something was wrong.

Eventually I called the camp and the coordinator said the bus would be late. But still things seemed incongruent, and when I called her back, she said it was the bus *to* Toronto that was late, not *from* Toronto, because that bus was not coming until Sunday the 13th, of course, not Saturday the 12th. We were a full 24 hours early, with me due to fly home later that afternoon, and check-in for my flight just hours away.

It was one of those times where you could just give up on life, you tried so hard to play it cool.

We shuttled back to the hotel, ordered fancy pastries and hot chocolate. When I finally got the airline on the phone, they were no help in searching for the answers as to why my life had come to this, why I always got things so wrong, got the camp dates wrong, got the husband wrong.

Sometimes, could I not just get what I paid for?

Luckily my big brother, who lived in Toronto and had shepherded me through the separation, had the same propensity for overplanning that I did, and the carefree nature to handle any catastrophe. Before we knew it, he was coming for Goose, and together they planned a boys' night of swimming and pizzas, and they told me to get lost, and go back to where I came from, and that they would take it from here.

When given the time and space, behind a five-ounce airport merlot, I started to write. I would start over. I would make something new. I would give myself permission to fail, over and over. I was an electron; I was a light wave.

And when I got home, I breathed deeply and threw the contents of my suitcase on the floor, in a grand gesture, and saw something shift in the bottom. When I opened the hidden pocket, something fell out. The book's pink cover glittered with golden stars. Daydreams.

My words, the story, my testimony. It had been with me all along.

With love and light,

Mo Duffy ~~Cobb~~

act one: exploding stars

WHERE YOU AND I EXPLODE

where you and i explode
into radiant white light

astral

When my marriage disappeared, for a while, so did I. Family dinners, lemonade stands, kids on bikes with scraped knees. A kiss when he got home from work. *What are we doing on Friday? Is Sunday with your folks?* Vacations, vaccinations, oil changes. All gone.

I had this recurring image of my life, as if I'd seen it explode with my own eyes. There was nothing left, except radiant white light.

There is energy in explosion. Energy is transformed, not removed. Changed, not broken. If my deep dive into quantum mechanics in my twenties had taught me anything, it was that. The Law of Conservation of Energy. As an over-electrical being with epilepsy, it was something that I thought about a lot, on a loop sometimes. When energy explodes, what is left, what is left?

I don't know if it was all the *Planet Earth* I watched as a young adult, or what exactly started to happen, but all of a sudden I became the rush of a wing, the trail of a monarch's migration from Canada down to Mexico, the breath of a dragonfly or the salt in the air.

Mitchell would sometimes tell me that I was a being who floated above the clouds, on a pink balloon, and his only job was to keep and hold the string. It always gave me great comfort to know that he recognized that I belonged to a different stratosphere; I was more of the heavens than of the earth, perhaps.

I've always been more comfortable in an astral setting. So when the ground started shifting, and I felt lost, or alone, or misunderstood or desperate, I would just say, *Radiant. White. Light.* The words somehow became my fierce protector, my talisman, my words to live by.

Part of me is still writing astrology in my head, a throwback to my first ever column in the *Saint Mary's Journal*, "Astrological Mojo."

> *As she was born on the eighth of December, she exercises a continuous balance between the materialistic and the spiritual; she is infinity, she is white light.*

And somehow, the world started to make sense again, like how fire needs air to breathe, how water is pulled by the gravitational forces of the moon.

in this sphere or the next
i am radiant white light

interstellar

When life fell apart, I started nightly affirmations with the kids, so they would know in their souls that they had a guide. We practiced them each night, made them up to feel strong, to feel awake, to feel like we were wrapped in poetics and philosophy and stars and not a tidal wave that was coming to consume our house, swallowed in the belly of a whale.

Never the same, but to begin, we would acknowledge the journey. *I am a traveller, I am the road.* And then usually follow it up with *I am the journey, I am the destination.* They might begin to shift under their blankets, with the moons on their ceilings, ask a question or jump in with one of their own. *Speaking of travelling, could they walk tomorrow, instead of taking the bus?*

I wanted them to talk. I wanted them to share. *I am a suitcase, I hold space.* "When Mom and Dad were together," I would hear them say to their friends. "It's going to be two houses now," they would say. "It's going to be different, but it's going to be okay." Friends nodding in agreement. "Sounds cool," they would say. The resilience of littles shows up everywhere, and I begin to learn from them.

Give them back to their power now. *I am a maker, I am a creator. I am a cup to be filled. I am kindness, I am light.* Notice movement, notice change. Acknowledge, acknowledge, acknowledge. *I am a river, and I am the rocks that the water flows over.*

I would always go interstellar to close, to know that wherever they were, we were always under the same moon, that the planet was so small, and we were small too. *I am a bridge to the stars. I am the skyline. I am the eagle that flies to the tops of the trees.*

They didn't have prayers, but they had something.

you can't hurt me,
i am radiant white light

a new prescription

When there is grief, it follows you around. It's at the farmer's market, at the superstore. It comes to parties, to Thanksgiving dinner, to Mom's, to your best friend's house. And it definitely shows up at the eye doctor.

Just look through, and tell me, she said.
Better in 2, clearer in 3. Click, click.
We can change the focus, adjust the lens.

Can I become my own transformation; can I adjust the lens?
That seems all our own. We'll dream the highest dreams and visualize the clouds above us. Better in 3, clearer in 4. Click, click.

Walking on broken glass, we can move through the anger, feel the waves of pain. Climb up through the realm to a place where we are still connected. Better in 4, clearer in 5. Click, click. A new way, with new goals, the smiles of our children, adding up the days on our calendar.

Read the big E. Strain if you need to. Parenting is teamwork, collaboration, structure, organization, and discipline. Nothing's changed there, right? *Your eyes have improved*, the optometrist says. *But you'll need reading glasses when you're older.*

you can’t see me
i am radiant white light

culture shift

At the coffee shop, the end of the bar.
In the lineup for milk, the school parking lot.

It seems everyone wants to "get the story straight."
Judgment comes swiftly,
and I leave the conversation feeling wounded.

An aura of responsibility in the air, I still feel protective, defensive.
That's my husband you're talking about.

Ex-husband, they say.

I think carefully about what to say next.
It seems the role has shifted, regardless of the private pain of loss,
we hold the added weight of being cultural soldiers

to educate the masses that some endings can be beautiful.

But the toll of cultural re-framing is high,
and it feels like some days the battle cannot be won.
The path to peace is riddled with landmines and

while no one gets gold stars for the way they
handled their marital separation,

some days, it feels that there is
the expectation
that you should.

the truth cannot hurt me, if
i am radiant white light

continental

A small hotel lobby somewhere in New Brunswick
cheap tables and a stupid wooden fork
the coffee's hot but I'm uncomfortably close to others
then all of a sudden, the enlightenment begins.

A woman to a man, "How long was your first marriage?"
with a short follow up, "How many kids you got?"

like someday this phase I'm in will be a long and rested dream
where we peacefully transitioned from one state to the next.

Rebirth or afterlife? Hard to know what poetic descriptor might fit.
I pull a muffin apart, push jam around my plate.

Rebirth gives us all a new chance, but
afterlife suggests we had a life together that is now gone.

The sage smoke rises to the wind.
Afterbirth is messy. Afterbirth hurts.
What is over, what has changed?
A baby has been born.

What has been here, today?
It's the end of an era, beginning of an age.

Co-parenting ticks the boxes: you have a pickup time, I have a phone number. We can meet on the field if we need to.

But what more? We've left the silk nighties behind.
We've left your Miami trips. We've left my non-profit boards.
We've left the stuff we *had* to do. *Had* to work around.

I almost forget what was in the middle.

Kisses stolen in the kitchen, sideways glances at the end of the night,
scallops, sizzling hot in the oven, glances up from lazy morning reading,
long drives to take in the sun setting on the north shore.

The rebirth chapter makes dreams for one, leaves blank space on the page
but it's a new language to learn and sometimes co-partnership seems
like a boring second place to the great and wild love we had.

The demotion hurts a little, continents drifting apart.
I could never have been enough for you, or was I for a while?

a glow around the moon
i am radiant white light

embers

a campfire for two
where you sang your heart out
shared your secrets

felt perfect
felt the bliss

a long road together
with vows and all that
the good and the bad
wove the years of love together into
magnificent tapestries

now the song is over
and suddenly
i am left to dance

alone

in the middle of a red-hot fire
i am radiant white light

linked

Words matter. They did before,
they do now, even more.
Maybe if we avoid certain topics
it would be better.

Your issue.

My issue.

The things I wouldn't do, the things you couldn't.

The hoops we still need to jump
through. Our unfinished business haunts
half-lit rooms.
Our plans
our blueprints frozen
in the middle of our next big dream.
The babies we love will keep us
together, but only when we figure out
how to be on the seesaw again.

To give and to take and to do it
simply without effort of tone,
complication, punctuation, broken hearts.

over time, over distance
i am radiant white light

weathervane

An unclear location. I turn in circles in the wind. How do I find true north, or should I look for another direction? When there are no clear roads, I wait for signs.

Intuitive directions, flying off the maps, just this once.

There are tools to help me figure out where I am—mindfulness and long walks and craft beer tours. Park playdates, my feet on sand. Planted.

Buckets of water, towels wet from the beach, cleaning ice cream off the floor of the car, and suddenly it feels like I've lost everything, the laughter of children, the place where everything made sense.

Dancing in the kitchen to the *Frozen* hits, cheeks sunkissed, the smoke from a barbeque and burgers on the grill, family family family.

The oldest practicing her firebirds, bike rides in the national park, packing lunches for field trips.

The smell of coconut sunscreen, reading and audiobooks and writing, practical gratitude, birthdays and body glitter, reflecting under the lights on the dance floor.

Excuse me, but how do I get back to the beginning?

i can see you
i am radiant white light

the
moment
when
you
realize
that some
things
are not
meant
to
last
a lifetime

counting moments, counting stars
i'm radiant white light

the breath that holds

Can you die from loneliness, standing in your kitchen
when the emptiness weighs you down
as though you had eaten
                                        stones?

Sinking you, further and further down
your eyes cast low, it hurts you physically
with no measures, to lighten yourself.

You grab an apple and a knife
you curl around the pain
hold your belly, but it is crushing,
it's not even identifiable.

Is it *something*?
Or the *lack of* something?
The weight of a tortured soul.

Will it be filled again, and how and with what?
You begin to peel, a fury, a rage
a toast to better days, your youth already spent

you feign guilt, feign regret.

Peeling faster, it fills the emptiness with
the spray from an apple, you cut the seeds out.
When you forget the unforgettable
sad sighs will once again be wild laughs
time will revolve
the world on its axis, but for now
there is only the breath that holds
the untruths you were deceived by

and you can pare the tension
with a deliberate practiced hand.

what happened next

Single lane traffic, passing on a blind curve,
I hold the vulnerability, the
heartbreaking indecision of what to do next.
In tarot, the lovers fill the spread.

surrounded by complication, the
the numbers don't add up,

but it feels a creative space.

Reasonable accountability?

Blinding pleasure in times of strife, calculations gone away. Missing digits here.

Mind bending guilt.
Even I feel like a perpetrator
any time we are together.
Justice, fairness, equilibrium,
scenarios with devastated results on both sides.

You keep your eyes on the road, blink hard to keep the tears back.

Can pain shield us from responsibility,
shame bending light backwards, to see its reflection
a retraction of light on the road.
Mixology turns red drinks purple, if you add blue curacao.

Driving past old PEI barns.
The barn's burning down.
Nails are hot. Nails are melting.

Moving forward, moving back
chess pieces in a strategic attack
the devolution of relationships' central topics.

Seeking clarity, seeking connection.
We must re-frame.

ritual of the daily

When you're going through a life change,
narrative is everything.

Just keep doing the things that get you through the day.
You're moving, so pack.

The kids are going to school tomorrow,
so go grocery shopping and make their lunches.

You do have a job, you know,
so get out the timeline and write back-cover copy.

Lei's friends are all here, and the prom is coming up.
Order butter chicken and call it a girls' night.

You're alone for a holiday,
so get adopted by a new family where you always belong.

Tuesday is coming and it's the first of the month.
Get your recycling out. Clean the garage while you're at it.

You want to go out with some girls you haven't seen in a while.
Practice in the mirror: "I'd really like to keep this personal."

You're remortgaging the house.
Time to do a deep dive into your financial picture.

Why can't you and Daddy live together anymore?
Honey, Daddy and I will always love each other and there are magical possibilities out there for us as a family.

Mom, are you okay?
Yes, I am Radiant. White. Light.

when nothing has changed
there is radiant. white. light.

bunk beds

The year before we separated, we bought a house together.

Intention is a beautiful thing.

We had been growing out of our old house for some time, with its small closets, slanted walls, and leaky basement. When we signed the papers for the new house in April, we felt a new energy, hopeful and vibrant, although we had no clue as to what the future held for us, exactly.

That fall, we gutted it—took down all the walls and began drafting the process of the interior rebuild. We imagined plenty of space for the kids, for cookbooks, for plants.

We would grow old together.

There were some pleasant surprises in the neighbours. Laura was a global health worker and my friend for over twenty years. When she got Covid in March 2020 and almost died, she packed up her family from Geneva and decided it was time to head back to PEI. Turns out, she bought a house three away from the one we bought.

But plans changed.

She witnessed the dissolution of the marriage firsthand, and together as rowdy girlfriends, we looked for a private venue to secure the unbecoming. The new house seemed a perfect fit for the job; the contractors had abandoned it for the winter.

No heat, no running water, and no electricity. No one would ever know we were there.

As the January winds blew around the dead-end street, no one even noticed that the driveway was unploughed, and the snow drifts reached so high we could barely get in the front door.

The only actual piece of furniture at the construction site was a set of bunk beds in the top southwest corner of the home, left there by the realtor. Our youngest daughter, a visionary, carefully planned the mermaid colours and other inspirations around this canopy-bunk centerpiece—so we negotiated their remainder. The bunk beds would stay.

Witness. Testify.

The Mermaid Room. It was kind of what I needed at the time, a private place to solve all of the world's problems.

When Laura and I started to use the empty house as our own private therapy getaway, the bunk beds got some good use. Laura and I received a sympathetic altruist in her husband, who began to deliver the comforts of home to the Mermaid Room. First appeared a battery-powered heater. Next, two lawn chairs and a small table. Fruity witbiers. Salami, then cheese.

It took time for Mitch to tell his family and friends his news. He liked guys. Maybe he had always had.

When he was ready, he said I could tell one person, and that was Laura. At first, we thought that we may be able to live together in a new capacity. Would we still be married, if we had new partners? I googled mixed-orientation marriages and dreamed up scenarios where we all lived in the house together. I fought against convention, tradition, against the expectations of cultural norms. I fought against the idea of "being divorced." We could reinvent the wheel, right?

It sounds crazy now, but at the time, we talked about it like things wouldn't necessarily change—much. I loved him for being brave enough to live his truth. He loved me for understanding. We loved the kids. Nothing would ever change.

"Jesus fuck, Mo," said Laura one night as we sat in our snow pants. "You should listen to yourself. It's like you're in the middle of a cholera outbreak, in a pandemic, and you won't wear your mask or put your gloves on. You have to look out for yourself, too, sometimes, you know?"

Nothing made sense anymore. When he travelled for work, and in this space apart, new questions circulated. I began to ask myself, *What do you want this new life to look like?*

And I waited for the answers.

the place we're all dreaming of
radiant white light

tectonic

When I wake up, postictal, there is an ambulance in the driveway. The kids have called the neighbours, called my friends.

Mom has left the room.

It's my seventeenth wedding anniversary, and all day I have been thinking about devotion. What is it, what does it mean?

And it's just all been a little too much, because a seizure comes and catapults me straight into the planet's magnetic forces, into the same energy that shifts tectonic plates and creates landslides, bubbles volcanoes over.

Radiant. White. Light.

Do you know the day? the EMT asks. *The prime minister*?

My husband, he's... he's... I can't get the words out.

They're recently separated, the oldest chimes in, pats my face down with a facecloth. Her expression says, *Come back Mom, the littles are worried about you.*

Whether it was stress, or an interruption in meds, or the anniversary, I can't explain away the things that I am holding right now.
space | the reigns | the kids | grief | a business | a house | my sanity | dysfunction | recompense

The top of a business letter between myself and the stars.
Everything at once.

Dad is on the phone now, he's in the car heading to Nova Scotia, did we want him to turn back?
I pull a Nana and say, *Oh no, dear, not on my behalf.*

In numerology, seventeen is seven plus one, which is eight, the number of infinity, and balance in the spiritual world.

Forces beyond me at work here.
It is time to reset.

i’m not here,
i’m radiant white light

act two: deep space

A QUESTION OF WHERE WE ARE

when you're a light wave

when you're a light wave
you can bend and shift, you can be long or be short
you're just you
livin' the light wave life

you look different in different settings
you can reflect and bounce off surfaces
head somewhere new
let your surprise and your curiosity guide you
or refract when you travel from medium to medium
vary in contrast under an ocean wave
a new perspective
but always shining your own way

you diffract
hide under beds
sneak through tiny passages
even when you get lost from your group
you never feel less than whole

you flourish even in interference
find a way to go around
unfazed by the darkness of mystery
just another friend
that helps you find your way out

the biggest card to play
is that you're both a particle and a wave
the gun and the smoke behind it
the camera and the picture
stop bath and fixer and time
alive in the present moment
always in the perfect transition

no existential crises
no judgement
just existing where you are

but if you need to go
all parties agree that
you can get out fast
299,792,458 metres per second
the universal constant
the speed of light

it could be you

"The position of rebound is filled,"
she laughed, on a Monday
as we walked the dogs towards the lighthouse.
The girlfriends and the dog walkers have been there for it all.

How better to explain a weekend of desire,
feeling wanted, feeling full, for the first time in forever,
the creation of options in physical connection.

They say German Shepherds have better senses,
can see in the dark, can find and know illness and death.

What can he tell me now—how do I go forward?
We can't go back.

The concept of selection, of choice.
People say it's the open road, that the perfect mate is out there
so get out there and find that person.

But I don't believe that anymore.
There is only attraction, vulnerability
and the urgency of heat.

But my dreams were full of questions, filled with danger,
a squid's ink blasted through the water.

Somehow, under water.
Somehow, marked.

alone or together
in radiant white light

behind anyway

Laura and I are in the backyard again.
She asks me, "What's behind it, when you say *anyway*?"

Behind anyway is the urgency for things to be normal, transfixed.
No more tears in the kitchen when I don't expect them.

No more explanations of what happened, what he knew, when,
whether or not I suspected this or could I have known that.
We are not hypotheticals, we are beings
with emotional spectrums that need the tender care of holding.

Behind anyway
there is an uncomplicated place of comfort, of security.

Behind anyway, people are not lost, but found.
They know who they are, they know where they belong.

They are travellers, and they follow the stars instead of
forgetting to look up.

how to turn rage into lemon squares

When confusion was over, anger took hold.

They say, make lemonade. They say, be sweet. Be honest, they say. With teenagers, even. With a gay husband, even. With accountants, even. Be still. Be predictable. Wear an apron. Drink your tea. Be stable. Be well. Do the work. They work, they say. Oh the enlightened. Thank you for the inspiration that yoga can show me the way. Or green tea. Or meditation. Or breath work. These levels of judgement. Of doing the right thing. You did the wrong thing. You're still doing the wrong thing. What you want is wrong. What you feel is wrong. Who you want is wrong. There has been a change of scope. It requires a new plan, a new deadline. New pricing. If you change your mind, you pay more. If you miss a deadline, you pay more.

The day I took my wedding rings off, I cried so much I couldn't see straight. My bathroom floor kept me company for a while. It was a nice, private place to fall apart. Three circles of white gold. Eleven diamonds. Four elements. One design. One circle, a ring of fire. One circle, with a tiny branch, the whole of the earth. Him with water and air.

When the teenagers found me, I was admittedly a little delirious. "Mom, what are you doing there?"

"Nothing, I'm..." I reached. "I'm making a list."

"What's your list for?" they asked, thinking I'd completely gone off my rocker. Which, of course, I had.

"I'm making lemon squares," I said. It was the first thing I could think of, and I just blurted it out.

"You're making lemon squares?" they repeated. "From the bathroom floor?"

"Yes, I'm making lemon squares."

If we've learned anything from *The Sound of Music*, it's that, as Fraulein Maria tells us, when the lord closes a door, somewhere he opens a window. Lemon squares would become my window. For weeks.

For starters, it can take you days to make them. First trip to the grocery store. Cold butter and flour for the shortbread crust. Setting the pastry overnight. Second trip to the grocery store. Lemon selection; becoming one with the lemons. Zesting. Squeezing for their juices. Third trip: powdered sugar, parchment paper.

Setting. Raspberry accoutrement. Temperature. Heat. Even a party at the end to bring them to.

The goal is that it takes you so long to make them, you have completely forgotten what you were upset about. I used the same technique when I quit smoking in my twenties, when I had outgrown teenage rebellion and was old enough to know better. Every time I wanted a cigarette, I would boil the water for tea. Flush a tea bag in there. Wave it around angrily. Drink it. I mean, it's probably why I still hate green tea, even when I try to love it. But I'm pretty sure I quit smoking. I mean, I quit for a while anyway.

I remember, I was reading about Zen at the time and planning my career as a clairvoyant. *Zen Buddhism: Selected Writings of D. T. Suzuki*. I must have learned the mediation technique there. I'm sure it has a technical Buddhist term. 'Zen no-mind' comes to mind.

So every time I got upset about the divorce, I just thought about lemon squares, and the kids were in love. They thought my lemon square kick was the best. Instead of asking me where Dad was, they started asking me questions about pastry, and what if I set it less than overnight, what would happen? Process.

I had piqued their interest with just enough sweetness, and it gave them a palette to talk about the other things on their minds; *How is a bisexual different from a heterosexual?* Very good question.

Let's leave that open ended. I could only write my own story; I could never try to write his. And with the newness my family was experiencing, the last thing I wanted to do was to box it in with language.

Could Daddy and Daddy's boyfriend live with us, if they wanted to? I think that Daddy and Daddy's friend need some privacy, maybe. Maybe Mommy does too. Uncertain. Pass the lemon juice.

Texture. Sugar. Why is *accoutrement* always in French? Could they come to the party? When would they know if they could come to the party? Could they just taste the squares, then, just in case?

The littles were fooled, but the teenager wasn't. If I came home with lemons, she started to pace. Was everything okay, did I see him again? What had transpired, was there an event? Was there a need for the raspberries? Would I need to zest lemons, could she call someone for me? Maybe a wine night with Laura or Gen?

I only actually made them twice, maybe three times, but in my head, I made them for months. And it was the best goddamn distraction that I had ever, ever created. I didn't even need to make them anymore, I just needed lemon juice in the house in case I wanted to make them in the middle of the night. I could just wash a pan and leave it out.

The winter passed. The spring passed. The word got out. I didn't have panic attacks in the grocery store anymore or patch too many words together when I saw inquiring neighbours. I calmed my brothers down. I over-explained things to the aunties. I was still around. He was around. Things were going to be... *fine*.

Life went on. And in all of life's tartness, I made lemon squares. Sometimes violently, sometimes in tears, sometimes I just repeated, "Lemon squares, lemon squares, lemon squares," with my head under a blanket.

We were going to get through this. With lemons, with butter, and with icing sugar.

re-train

There is no we, she says. There is only you, and there's him.
And you can answer for yourselves.
A meditator with sweet intentions.
I feel like an old horse gone back for re-training.

Come on neural pathways, save me now.

I sit in the silence of confusion.
I can't stop saying *we*. Even when I try to stop, I can't.

For as long as I can remember, we have been we.
One team. One family. One unit.
Pizza family movie night, back-to-school, Christmas.
March break we're running together at the airport,
summer's here again.

We've worked together, for each other.
We know each other's plays. Committee work, dance drop-off,
taco nights, yoga and the gym.

Does that need to change now? Just because we're sleeping

in separate rooms, in separate houses, on separate roads?
The same maples overhang, the same birches. The clouds, the salt air.
One week after school the bikes go east, one week after school they go west.

We may not be the old we,
but we are not broken.

Maybe we can look different.

As Goose says, "Pause game." It's time for a grilled cheese, a glass of milk.
Bring sustenance before you bring conclusions. Bring reflection. Become inspired.
No one can tell us there's no we. We will create our own point systems, clarity and boxes going forward.

I can check them for him, he can check them for me.
Somedays it feels like chess, but somedays it feels
like together, we are playing against the computer.

breathe into it now,
you are radiant white light

momcation

When the days began when the kids were with Daddy, I became kind of at a loss. What would I be, when I wasn't a mom? The first few times I spent the days by myself, it was an odd kind of stress. No homework, no Brownies, no soccer practice.

Write in the morning, write at night. Walk the beaches, go for drives. Go to yoga whenever I wanted. See the girls, admittedly, a lot. Soon the fridge was stocked with cheeses, beers. Charcuterie for dinner every night.

I roamed around downtown, enjoyed the nightlife, until boys began to hit on me, then I stopped. Whatever I wanted, I didn't want that.

When summer came, I decided to head down to Maine on a road trip, to see Phish, an old favorite from back in my pre-married days. It's funny that the word *single* doesn't even come to mind. Pre-married. Like everything in the world revolved around the sixteen years of together-ness I shared coat racks and cereal cupboards with a man. What about before? What about after?

I pulled out maps and ferry schedules. I made playlists and packed the car with bathing suits, blankets and books, hiking boots and towels and homemade power balls.

I hadn't gone travelling alone since what felt like the beginning of time.

When I drove out North River Road with the windows down, a box of egg salad sandwiches and dill pickles that my father packed beside me, I breathed deeply. I felt new somehow.

Maybe this was a clean slate, a new beginning. Maybe it was all meant to be—the stars, the cosmos, lining up for me. But I wouldn't have done anything differently, right?

Deep dives into your past can be dangerous, but life transitions are rife with them. I had secured the most wonderful therapist, Claire, whom the girls nicknamed Claire-ity. She brought me back to long-forgotten places in my life. *Tell me about the first time you didn't feel like you were enough.* All of a sudden I was back to pigtails in church with a too-short sweater and Mom rolling her eyes.

She rolled me through all my life's complications, back to simpler times, and together, we looked for my power. If I found it, could I have it back please? I was a kale leaf, massaged with olive oil and flash cooked. Could I be palatable, again?

When I got to Portland I got to see my beautiful friends, one of whom is a jewellery maker. We sat down, and she said, *Let's talk about the rings.* There would be more, and they would be mine alone. The only thing I wanted was for them to be broken; open rings create space for the present, space for the future.

I made the time and space to do the trip my way. Wharfs in Saint Andrews, wharfs in Portland, wharfs in Lunenburg. Kites and the voices of best friends I hadn't seen in ten years.

You never needed him Mo, and the world needs you now, so you have to let him go.

i can travel through you
i'm radiant white light

saint john michael

there are no saints anymore but there should be
the post separation vulnerability
creating this fragile yellow corona around you
visible to all those who you may encounter

it's too bad you can't order a
a sphere of protection online
with your sharpies and glue
now, newly impenetrable!

but when you are vulnerable you need protectors
gorillas in the mist

it's a different space for a woman to be
extracted from a marriage, taken out like an FBI operative
there is the sudden urge for others to protect me
and many of the bros in my life swooped in

the look in their eyes
either pity or shame
or just that they wanted to hold me

blessed in the power i had around me
the circle held strong
listened and held space

the bros didn't pretend it was going to all be okay
they shared their own pains along the way
with pickups full of wood, with generators during the storms,
and trucks to carry my bikes when i had too many

to shine a light in the darkness
prepared to talk all night if they had to

once
mitch told me
that
i
would
always
be
his
wife
because
he would
never have
another
one

these days[1]

When you have a new idea, meaningful work begins.
Study art. Be creative and figure out what you're good at.
Teach communications, start to write reviews and essays,
travel blogs. Network and start to make a few friends in high places.

I hope someday we'll sit down together
and laugh with each other 'bout these days, these days

Study language, practice form.
Bend genre, build new structure.

Re-vise,
re-vision,
re-quest.

There are chapters now. Add research.
What did it smell like in Bangkok on Chinese New Year?
The realization comes that it's a memoir.

---

[1] Inspired by "These Days" by Rudimental, Ft. Jess Glynne, Macklemore & Dan Caplen

The first book launch, with tears of joy, and fear and trepidation.
The hugs that followed when you let it go to the world
and then more stories, wild imagination then the development of intent.

We were gonna move to Brooklyn, you were gonna study art.

Someone asked me once, "How do you write?"
A cheeky question, like maybe you might not dare to answer it,
like the ideas might hear you and not come back.

The ideas, they wake you up at night,
they follow you around during the day,
when you write them down, they leave you alone.

You were the light for me to find my truth.
I just wanna say, thank you.

But then you are enveloped by them and suddenly
your words are all around you.
They're on the wall, they're in essays, they're splattered over books,
they're on sticky notes, they're by your bedside.

Cigarettes in the ashtray
Reminiscing on those past days
I thought you'd end up with my last name
But that changed
And I travelled around the world, think where you living at now?

Creativity began to burn a light in the dark for me;
You're never alone if you have its heartbeat in the room

It's not moving up, exactly. It's moving on from one thing to another.
First an executive director, then a chair, then a writer, then a leader.
First a writer, then a coach, pouncing forward, falling back, missteps.

Mantras, mantras, mantras.
"There are no wrong turns, only unexpected destinations."
"All I need is within me."

When you don't know the answers,
all you have is the trust of the process.
When the beat is there, the notes are there
and the rhythm is there, the song can come together.

Love is just a tool to remind us who we are
and that we are not alone when we're walking in the dark.

i am a powerful force
i am radiant white light

in the balance

What does it mean to live your truth? It means to be whole. I. AM. WHOLE. Say it with me.
i. am. whole.

When you let go too fast, what's left?

The fire of Sagittarius. A manifesting generator. I read somewhere, "Watching it burn with the match in his hand." That feels apt. A new grasp on perfection, or whatever it is, it has me holding on for dear life.

Momentum builds, and I gain equilibrium. There are moments of personal growth in the chaos, steadiness. I'm feeling things I haven't felt in years. I want something new, now, something I've never had before. What is the currency, and what is the change?

Or is it only truth that I want? Your truth, my truth, in symbiotic harmonies? It is a new plateau with its shifting grounds that kicks me to my knees sometimes, but when I stand, I can see for miles, and the sunrise is gorgeous.

I decide I like it exactly how it is, with just a shade more freedom.

More candlelight, more wine. Music, parties and playlists. Lazy mornings, adventure and more of my time to take. It is spontaneity, it is Sundays, it is Tuesdays. It is early in the morning, it is late at night.

It is less shifting in the kitchen, less nervous tensions. Less red lights and sleep timers. Less vitamins, less measurements, and less precision. Less structure, less self-obsession.

Breathe in the change. It is more lectures, more culture. More concerts, long walks, and time when no one is looking for me. More sharing, more playfulness, more memoir. The permission to be doing what I need to be doing. More big picture, more long term.

Less walking the path alone, wondering what. Wondering why. Maybe now—we know.

when you know, you know

"No is a complete sentence." —Jane Fonda

Trust the process was getting a little old.

Sometimes it takes a nineteen-year-old to show you the way.
Leila recently started saying, "When you know, you know."

We were talking of friendship, which can be complicated and troubled at times.
But *when you know, you know* covers a lot of territory.

It says, *I believe you*. It says, *You have permission*.
It says, *Please feel what you feel and express it as you see fit*.
It says, *You are secure*. It says, *It's all been brought to the light*.

In a way, it is *trust the process*'s enlightened older sister.

An old friend dropped off a card yesterday, wrapped in a pink ribbon.
Her letter, handwritten, finished with, *Look for the gifts.*

Look for the gifts is like the old, wise grandma.
She practices gratitude wherever she goes.

divorce is on instagram

there's plenty of advice out there
for those who need to hear it
and also for those who don't

there's a reason they call it
doom scrolling

people peddling their wares
in an overcrowded marketplace
coaches can walk you along a ways
the boundary builders sell their books
the makers offer homemade printables
for your complete divorce success
and crystals and retreats want to help you start again

the water is rising, rising

trying to be careful where I look for inspiration
needing not retreats but the
poetry and music can build the connections that sustain me

i fill the channels with
octopuses and world health and
the glistening snow dust of weathermen
whole accounts dedicated to dads who sing acapella
and farmers who walk with tiny lambs

the good of the world is out there
if you can only stay long enough to find it
i breathe into pure intentions—
and hope the algorithm will show me
the path forward

walking
waking
joyfully

i am the message
i am radiant white light

superstore

when a bad day comes, it really comes
the grief eats you alive, the torment of change

you're in the grocery line
when someone asks you how you are

banana, grapes, strawberries, milk
and the wind gets knocked out of you
you're down on the field

beep beep beep beep
reverberations of shock and pause
uncomfortable, for a moment

you'd die for a cosmic portal
to scoop you up and out of here
you shouldn't be in public
could the goddesses of marital separation
not have protected you

you fumble in your purse for a wallet or a card

and you look up and into darkness
like the power is out, it's a full system shut-down
and your balance is lost

your mind goes to vacancy, when all of a sudden
the goddesses do give you a sign

they remind you that there is bubblemint gum in the world
and flowers and love and summer rain

and in a show of strength you smile, say some words
like how good you are, the kids, perfectly well, perfectly well

and when it's over
you know in the dark you can see the stars
that everything returns in time
that you're better now
and so is he

the tarot of the rings

dark bar with a girlfriend
we sit on church pews, reflection of
a single candle in the window
here comes the spread

it's the scales of justice again
the princess out on a rowdy evening
the wheel of fortune
a direction that hangs in the balance

the death card signals an ending
but on deeper look, rebirth
do spreads bring questions
or do questions bring the spreads

eagles in the treetops
warmth of the sun
when you believe that you can
transform—shed your skin like a snake

the girl who is forged in fire
can sink into the unknown

a fast and moving universe
you are radiant white light

separation agreement

"Do you want to be happy, or do you want to be right?"
—Deepak Chopra

In the fall, one of the literary magazines put out a call for submissions: the things that keep you up at night. I froze, in actual terror. Something *was* keeping me up at night. The separation agreement.

First of all, I wrote it alone, which he didn't like. "It's just a draft," I said. "I'm just getting it started." And then, "It's a google doc," I added. "It's live."

It made promises neither of us knew how to keep. We loved our children, but did we "promise" to be good parents? We promised to be fair, to share, to mediate with help if need be. We would swing back and forth through Christmas and birthdays, host open discussion forums around special events. On paper, it was all very diplomatic.

There was no *who will clean out the garage when you move? How will one of us feel to see the art on the other's walls?* The gears of unoiled machinery and sticky things.

The proceedings were growing long, and I was tired. I coped with my parents' disappointment. The marriage was over, and I tried my best to keep them uninvolved. I heard myself saying things like, "The separation is moving along," and "We've got some really good people on it," like we were producing a film, with actors and timelines. Sometimes I was the director, and sometimes he was.

I asked for more, then he asked for more—a process of scathing indifference. A cutting, difficult process of grief, of finding light under darkness. My philosophy of finding tolerance was tested in new, absurd ways. Repulsed by a world where my marriage was adding up to numbers and dollar signs, I felt exposed, minimized.

The divorce literature tells you, *Never cut what you can untie*. We were never dollars and cents, and we knew that.

We were still in shock together, in love, not knowing how to leave each other, planning a divorce party. Wouldn't it be fun to get the old gang together again?

Like nothing had really changed.

But through the spring, working with the lawyers and the accountants, we waited for revelation to come, our lives simply reduced to words like "asset mix," our homes, where our children learned to walk, just lines on a balance sheet.

Even as I was consumed by it, I missed the deadline to submit.

you can't hurt me,
i'm radiant white light

backspace

Writing notes to teachers used to be easy,
but now it's an existential crisis.

My husband,
Backspace backspace.

My ex-husband,
Backspace backspace

My wasband,
Backspace backspace

My former partner,
Backspace backspace

Veda's father,
That he will never not be.

soggy fries

Two girls who danced in the rain
We called each other best friends
A light in the dark for the other
Taxis and parties and airplanes
I couldn't have lived without you

You put meals in front of my kids
Cared for them like they were your own
Emptied the dishwasher at the end of the night
I couldn't have lived without you

Dismantled our relationships at the same time
Carried each other through the dark
Wine glasses, craft nights, and grief books
I couldn't have lived without you

Once he kissed me in the kitchen
Startled me, held me
In a time of chaotic disruption
I couldn't have lived without him

Cried in the car and at the end of the bar
A complicated belonging amidst the betrayal
We put the wood in for the winter
I couldn't have lived without him

Lined up to take sides, the allies divide
No one but us left in the room
With the laughter of ghosts
I couldn't have lived without him

The road to forgiveness is long
A story too forlorn to tell
From the river to wild ocean seaway
We'll bid all the stardust farewell

"Out beyond ideas of
wrongdoing and
rightdoing,
there is a field.
I'll meet you there."

—Rumi

manifest

The relationship books have arrived. The self-help trend is in full force. Every book, a companion podcast, companion website, companion workbook.

Dream up the perfect partner, it says, and he will be there. The lines to the universe are open. What does he look like?

Manifesting him, he is wise, untroubled. Adventurous, knows what he wants. Decisive. Someone who does not seem complicated, but who is intricately detailed.

Caretaker qualities. Can love frisbees and soccer games. Is creative and philosophical and reads interesting books, flipping pages by the fireside. Sometimes, he reads them to me.

He loves to cook, but washes dishes too, and shows up with steak and potatoes when my office hours run long. An understanding mate.

He loves to travel, and is a good citizen with a fulfilling job. He makes time for his mother, talks to babies, picks up toddlers and talks to them into a game of cards. He's a good friend.

Someone who writes, who can communicate. He likes to work outdoors, he gets dirty. He likes to camp and fish and sink into riverbeds. He is authentically himself.

Someone who is his true self. He makes mistakes, and carries his emotions well, most of the time. He loves the beach, even if it's getting late, because he wants to see another sunset. And he always packs the perfect picnic.

He slows me down when I need to sleep, shuts the door in soft morning light. He makes space for all moods, and can share me with children, teenagers, dogs, cats, parents, siblings, stories, and girlfriends—the Brighton moms, the yoga moms.

He reads poetry, and sometimes writes his own when he needs to. Loves animals and walking dogs in the woods, without being asked, being begged, or negotiated with.

He likes spontaneous stops, and sometimes, to not know where he is going.

Likes girls.

that first christmas

In late summer, we failed out of mediation. There's no we, anymore, Maureen, there's just you and there's him. I heard the words, but everything that came out of my mouth was still, we. I know, but we decided... I know, but when we talked about it... Yes, but we thought you should know. Practice saying I, she said. She had me slowly mouth the word. It was like teaching me a new language.

Yes, our lives were moving in different directions. Yes, he was going to be better. Yes, I was going to be better. Yes, he was going to find someone new. Yes, I was going to find someone new. We were going to become new constellations, radiant white light.

But after sixteen years, we certainly weren't going to let someone sitting in an office downtown tell us that there was no we anymore. We left her office. We went for lunch. He texted me later. I called. We wanted to hold our children in our shared community, values, and dreams. Turbulence in the marriage made us rethink the nuptials, but we never second guessed wanting to do right by each other. We would separate, we said, even if we had to do it together.

The teenager was off to college, the littlest ones finishing elementary school. They understood what was happening was for the greater good. At my house, they got mini muffins in an extra high cupboard. At his house, they got TVs in their rooms.

That fall, I practiced saying *I*. The days he kept the kids stretched long. I went to the grocery store, bought raspberries and baby carrots, that mozzarella that the little one really liked. I couldn't remember what an adult female's diet consisted of, living alone in the wild without her kin.

The more I talked to people, the more I started to encounter ruptures in the marital system. Stories poured of the fractured love of women who had aged out of the matrix. And in a stage of my life where I was supposed to be focusing on self-care, it was like vultures out there. The girls were furious. Who's taking the house? Have you signed the papers yet?

I repeated the story on an auto-loop. We had taught three children how to walk, and now we were going to teach each other how to fly. We had a brilliant marriage. We were going to be brilliant co-parents. The future seemed bright, even as we—in his words—had blown up our lives.

But as the community mourned the passing of our coupledom, I was left with a misplaced sense of grief. I'm so sorry, they said. That's terrible, they said. Friends scattered furiously to take sides. There are no sides, I argued, it's just what's best for everyone. But the rumour mill cranked out the stories, and people just lapped it up. And it began to hurt like it hadn't before.

And I have to admit, that first Christmas, things stung a little. We argued over the Christmas card. The kids picked the photos, I added a glittery trim, and it arrived in the mail. "The picture of us together is misleading," he said. "You can't send it out." Furthermore, he asked me to trim my list, leave his family out of it and take "his friends" off, twenty-long friendships he planned to disappear.

I wrote a holiday letter that was brilliant, honest, and raw, and didn't send it. The theme that was developing was that people needed a curated, presentable version of the truth. A casual dispatch, we like our mistletoe with a side of gingerbread and peppermint. We don't talk about the fudge that never set, the year we burned the chocolate. I knew I had to hit the Christmas card reset button, but I just didn't know how.

I felt lost in this new post-marriage relationship. Even though we had chosen this upper path of clarity and respect, it's like our culture wasn't ready for it. The responses were sharp-witted, pointed. Everyone had an angle. She really messed that up, didn't she? He couldn't have known, could he? Culture swarmed on the hot mess that was left, bees swarming to the hive. This caused heartbreak, caused division.

We broke down the holiday hour by hour, making sure each of our families had a share. It was the opposite of bringing families together, it was the systematic plan to tear a family apart. Checks and balances were installed at every stage of the way. Santa became a spreadsheet. The family traditions were hijacked by both of us. Blood pressure went up.

I would be wrong if I didn't admit that I made mistakes along the way. My hot temper got me into trouble more than a few times.

The impatience of transition clouded the paperwork, and the finite details of our separation agreement kept me awake at night. Sixteen years times three children, times many wonderful memories, times houses and businesses, minus arguments, minus power, and minus control, divided by two.

It would take time, but eventually we had to school our lawyers, too. Dear lawyers, here's what we would like to do. This season, always remember that you can keep the peace, and that there's always magic in the air for all those who can see it.

act three: fusion

WHERE NEW THINGS BEGIN TO FORM

when we all move on
into radiant white light

pink light

I didn't want to move in January
but we waited for the house,
waited for the doors, new maple and birch,
waited for the cabinets, machinery and heat.
Waited, waited, waited.

Rehoming is a verb, an action
to make home again.

Leaving an old home behind
a process of heartbreaking grace,
where we brought our babies home,
charted their growth on the wall.

Now the great unboxing,
what to keep and what to let go.
Needing the breath to find
comfort in the new.

Then, the great arrival
and suddenly the new is everything.

Pink morning light streams in new windows.

You're happy,
Goosy says.
You're different.

Together we are rising up
the honour of beginning again.

Someday it will feel like that.

i'm a window not a door
i'm radiant white light

self-care isn't being mean

when i write
i reserve the time for myself
reserve the space
now i make sure to take what you want
reclaim, reclaim, reclaim

what are you writing they ask
beautiful stories with lingering clouds
stars that make trails across the sky and
when the calf finds its way home

full of truth, full of beauty
and
all
the
light
of
dusk

the guilt of notions
that life was brooding, was resentful

how long could you feel
when suffocated by privilege
that you were never enough?

open up anew
in radiant white light

reawaken

warning
contents may have shifted during flight

when i was fragile you handled me with care
delicately and tenderly
kept me stable when i was wild energy

you were calm when i exploded
fire and the bomb squad on their way
we held each other carefully
in the way that crumbling people can
with everything at stake and everything to lose

then suddenly a shift
pulled into a dance at a wedding
a snowstorm through the mountains
toast in the morning for the littles
packing backpacks notes and lunches
five dollars for the book fair

until it became what normal people do

refracted but unbroken
i'm radiant white light

book fair

PART ONE

Even as things change, the past follows.
Hundreds of people gather, in crowds, at tables,

blueberry muffins and coffee,
opening up worlds with words, and art.

I sit at a table with a pen to sign,
the author next to me with a power memoir

black leather pants and no more fucks to give.
Divorce. Been there, done that, she says.

I never quite liked that expression.
You have no idea. I stop, my eyes glazing over

like anything could be the same
in the world between me and her.

Kids' books stacked up on the table,

librarians, networking, and pitches.

Vulnerable moments in unknown spaces—did I almost cry for a minute?
Suddenly she knew that I wasn't ready for her pep talk.

I didn't mean to shock you, the lady softened,
or sound like I didn't care. I nod, acquiesced for the moment.

I'm going to be fifty, she said, *and at that point,*
I won't take any shit from anybody.

She said I needed therapy, she continued.
My best friend squared me in the eye,
over small plates of gluten free cake.

I know what to do, I just don't want to do it, she said.

Sometimes people sharing their stories is
enough to help you
manifest your own way.

Gluten free cake is
just not worth it.

PART TWO

Not that she asked, but my therapy journey had been mixed so far.
We'd started as a couple, then I'd moved to someone downtown, in an office,
who told me I was fine.
Maybe you should write a book, she said.

Does some part of us want to stay stuck, I wonder.
Stuck in the pain? Self-pain? Victimhood?

Still, the lady talked.
But the only person I'm hurting by not changing, is myself.

I had said to him,
You have a person out there, and that person is not me.
Sometimes the ultimate realizations come with clarity, come with focus.
They are healing, they are centric.
Their truths stick to you and after you know, you can never go back.

I needed you and you needed me. We changed each other and we changed the world.
Through heaps of joy, and some of the most painful of days.
Destruction, haze, storms, confusion,
and being on fire.

Will I be 50, too, someday?
The teachers line up for their copies. I get my pen ready.
And then, will I not take any shit from anybody either?

PART THREE

There is danger in proclamation.

I tried being fruit on the same tree, but
I'm a different tree now, with different fruit.
I'm in a different season, on a different continent
and I never want to eat your fruit again.

It's time to find my own way.

I regain joy for a moment, remembering an instance.
Mom is having a midlife crisis, the teens say.

They know. They see it.

And thank you very much.
Yes, I fucking am.

And I'm so fucking thankful because it is

SAVING
MY LIFE.

And who can I dedicate this to? The Scarborough Library.
Thank you for reading.

am i a new star, if
i'm radiant white light?

middle earth

Back slowly away from the past.
As Joan Didion says, life changes in the instant.

To build a new pathology
raising consciousness, raising minds.
What happens next, she asks herself.

Red snapper.
Mom, just cook the red snapper.
It's okay that it was his favorite.

If you colour outside the lines enough,
do you move to the next picture?

Just keep playing to the centre. Middle earth. Middle earth.
Guidance office says that the kids are happy.
Let them be happy. Don't upset them.

My psychotherapist says I have an accommodation disorder,
the thing my mom worked the hardest to teach me.

But kindness has a voice, and I have listened to it over the years.
Her world a culture of service
where she has always put the needs of others first.

Motherhood is selfless like that.
It's quite boring, yet worlds of complexity

redirect the narrative
and explore the world of offerings, the world of sacrifice.

All the books on boundaries: instead of *I'm doing it for you*,
Ask me what I want. Appreciate that we want different things.
Stop assuming you know what everyone wants.

Ask questions, don't assume answers.
Learn new ways, new ways to understand—

but the how-to-move-on part is tricky.

damages

Confession hour with D. Tell me what you want. Tell me now.
Quebec City brings the serum of truth. You had a communication breakdown.
You couldn't be honest. Or do you just say this now, because she's gone?

We're living with the tension of running together,
bandits with the smoking gun.
Joy and pain.

Slow moments and the fast pace of critical care.
The ICU of relationships.

Everyone's been shot—
I've been shot. You've been shot.
He has, she has.

To have a near-death experience, you have to *nearly die*.
The tunnel. The light. The choice. The decision.
It's you. It's always you.

Be one big family in a mixed orientation marriage, sure.

Have a new boyfriend, sure.
Teens drinking in the basement underage, sure.
Boys sleeping over, sure.
Thousands over on the credit line, sure.

Things are starting to wash away, all in a flash, an instant.

If privacy waited on a landing, for a train, would it miss you?
Are we losing the intention of finding each other?
I'm sinking under the concepts of speed, timing, and justice.

I retreat into the subconsciousness.
What are you writing next? Nothing, if I can't find the words.
Nothing, if it doesn't make sense. Nothing, if I can't get it out.

It's time to restore order.
The martinis are at five o'clock,
by the backsplash, by the flowers.
Set the conditions. Set the tone. Set the mood.

Fixated on the damages
lost in the station

from all the platforms of the past
to our next stop, forgiveness.

what is in the centre
of radiant white light?

team jerseys

You need water to survive
on the soccer pitch, when it's mid-august and the sun hangs high in the sky.

We arranged to meet there, to do the changeover for the littles. They would be busy, wouldn't notice that one parent had been swapped for another, or that's what we told ourselves.

I waved to the other moms and dads, packing snacks for their toddlers, pushing toys off blankets, and gripped the arms of my blue camp chair.

His new partner was in town, and together they were having a beautiful unfolding.

The grass grew long in spots, seven-year-olds took their best shots in the nets, dribbled the ball around small plastic cones.

Practice for life. I would meet him, and I was brave, and I could do this.

I watched and waited, and after a while, I saw the Volkswagen pull up.

When J got out of the car, I saw myself in his big bold sunglasses. Dressed in orange, he had tanned skin and a smile that killed. They looked happy.

We exchanged pleasantries, the beginning of a long road together.
My husband—had a boyfriend.

I was happy for them,
that amidst the world's chaos,
its vulnerabilities and its unknowns

they had found each other.
You need love to survive, too
on the soccer pitch, when it's mid-August and the sun hangs high in the sky.

in the stillness of the unknown
there's radiant white light

a poet's guide to small form carpentry

Some assembly required, it says.
When you put a dresser together for a week, you own it. You built it.
You've carried the massive box in from the truck, you've set up a space to assemble.

First, I was like,
I'm going to find a man to do all of this. A retired carpenter who really loves building things.
Maybe I could pay him by the project.
Go ahead, I dare you to do that.

When that fails, for any of a number of reasons, like he's having surgery or he's visiting his son in Alberta,
then you decide,
Do it yourself.
Don't ask for help.
Don't be vulnerable.
Don't show weakness.

Just get the hammer, get the screws.
Follow the instructions, not given in life by the way, or marriage,

but in giant boxes full of corner desks, yes.
Armoires for the teenager. Tracks, mirrors,
drawers for Goose, six-panel bureaus for Vades.
Light fixtures, shelving above the laundry room,
foosball tables with endless men that will spill all over your living room floor.

Building gives you lots of time to think, so settle in.
I've had too many years of *not* doing it myself,
which didn't teach me lessons. It didn't give me tools.
We rushed to assemble things, created stress,
When you want the end too fast,
you make mistakes along the way

After you've put together a dozen things, in a not-a-carpenter-but-artist kind of way,

you begin to see the benchmarks in life,
like why Tom, the contractor who's been hanging around,
makes everything looks so easy.

Don't drop the box because you can damage the contents inside.

Dowels usually go first,
kept in place with tiny bits of glue,
and sometimes need a gentle
hammer to find their place.

There are lefts and rights to everything.

The top usually looks like the top, glazed or coated.
The bottom usually looks like the bottom, or somehow unfinished.
Locate all the markings where screws can go,
points of interest on the wood,
find the knowings of the beast.

Stickers come off pieces of wood and miniature bags of screws,
so you'll have to assess depths for yourself,
match screws to lengths and widths.
Nails are for finishing.

Tracks have to be *really straight* to carry a drawer.
They also have to be right side up.
Lots of things in the world can be upside down,
and it can even be cool sometimes,
like in Jack Johnson songs or turning chairs to make forts,
but not drawers, unfortunately. They don't like to be
and it's a repetitive job, so it looks easy, but don't let
drawer tracks fool you, they will not work upside down.

Put the thing together in your 3D mind,
and let the directions secure the understanding.
If directions are over fifty pages, then you might need a friend for stamina,
and outside assistance can be a life-saving force,
so you'll be happy you called in the SOS.

Never be afraid of the time it takes to build.
Days could run into a week

and you'll have to leave for a day job,
after school runs, parent–teacher or the gym.

Pep talk yourself if you need to.
You don't just want to build,
you want to have fun along the way.
Get the screwdrivers out, and guacamole and chips too.

Allen keys are your friend, and you'll need two sets,
imperial and metric.
Drills can be your happy place, especially for exterior work
like locks for gates and lighting.
Get the kids involved once you're past the part where
they can muck things up.
Building is a family thing,

show your daughter
how playful and fun building your world can be

and eventually, one day, you've built yourself a home.

first light

hope springs eternal, dad says
over coffee, eggs on toast

springs arrive after long winters
ice turns to water

bathed in the first lights of morning
on inkerman lane

the joys of summer
fade into the warmths of fall

furious nights stretch into
peaceful mornings
renewal and grace somehow return
to their normal variance

affirmations punctuated like highway signs
hartland new brunswick, the world's longest covered bridge

the world needs more peace, more tolerance,
dad says, his mouth full of blueberries

as we wash away yesterday and
welcome all that is to come

bunk beds (the reprise)

"It will be the mermaid room," she said. "Two walls pink for the mermaid, two walls green for the ocean, and the ceiling blue for the sky."

Reinvention is really something, isn't it.

I had made some decisions, too. As much as I wanted to see myself as a progressive thinker, I didn't want to live in a sexually fluid household, with my husband and his new partner, as much as the kids thought that was a great idea. I wanted a romantic relationship between one woman and one man. I didn't want swingers. I didn't want an open marriage. I didn't want mixed-orientation. I didn't want change. And that was all okay.

I wanted flowers in the backyard, a barbecue. I wanted hockey nets downstairs where the boys could play all winter, even if they wrecked the walls. I wanted hotel pools in March. I wanted endless summers with camping and firepits. I wanted stars.

When I realized I didn't have to be more than I was, more than I was ready for, or more than I was capable of, the shift began. The equilibrium set me free. There was no timeline to complete "the work," the deep dives into how to build boundaries, the emotional fallout when you failed to keep them. There was no waiting for an answer. There was no one even listening.

Yes, we were going to get divorced, and no, we were not the first people on the planet to do it.

First person ever to get a cat. Genevieve and I started using this expression after Laura got a cat. Noticing its habits, its patterns, and how it interacted with you. Deciding you were going to be the smartest cat mom, by never letting it roam free. Deciding you were going to conquer the litter box, by teaching it to use the bathroom downstairs. Never mind the fact that you paid ten thousand dollars to refurbish said bathroom. Isn't that an expensive litter box? No darling, you're brilliant.

Now, we use the expression all the time. It means nothing, but it means everything.

When I run my fingers along the walls of her room, I remember the mermaids. I remember the days of not knowing, a time period we now—almost—endearingly refer to as "the winter of what-the-fuck." When the days ran together, the snow flew, and each day brought some new swirling disaster.

How would we tell the kids? How would we tell our friends? How would we ever move on?

Now in the mermaid room, in the rear view.

fresh ink

for your seventeenth birthday
you wanted to get matching tattoos

we'd flown out to calgary, drove the highway to banff
watched the mountains fill the skies and
walked amongst the cedar giants
we belonged there, it felt right

it's a new chapter, mom, you said
wise beyond your years
the dust starting to settle now
repurposed and rehomed

we called dad on speaker to confirm
the plan was ocean waves to sky
you felt he should be a part of it
being the body art expert in the family

a pint at the spaghetti place
rose coloured rays touching all corners
of the square, where we put them

on the bends and folds of our arms

we laughed a little in anticipation
and cried a little after
new markers would become us
the earth fills the air

where the mountains turn to ocean
and baptism is by art

the gay dads

When we let go
and just dropped the pretenses,
we had joy.

One drink at the music festival,
a few laughs over the summer and
always remembering to put our little
Halloweener first,
even if for tonight
Barbie will be accompanied by Ken, and Ken's friend, Kevin.

All of a sudden,
fiction is fact, and
you want them both at your birthday party.

where we become each other,
in radiant white light

lanterns

How do you build a lantern, something to guide your way in the dark?
Reinvent the path, trust that it is there.

Feel the ground beneath you, it doesn't have to be perfect.
No matter what your shoes look like, your feet are still there to carry you.

Bumps and stones and gullies, the road can sometimes take you out,
but nothing panics more than darkness.

A torch can light the way, sparked with the fires of trust, vision, and faith.
Fire as a guidepost to lead the way, into the unknown.

We walk together, to a place we've never been
and hope that when we get there

there will be the smell of the ocean, salt spray in the air
and the feel of warm sand beneath our feet.

double rainbow

When we got to the campground, it was close to dark. It was closed. No cell service, scrappy internet. Finally, someone came to let us in, gave us wood, and showed us where to camp for the night. It started to rain, so now surely nothing would dry. Through the clouds, a double rainbow appeared. It was a vague light, through rain, but light nonetheless.

You talked about us becoming something. I filled the space with words. We seemed to talk in circles these days, but every once in a while it turned to new beginnings.

Together that summer, we became the salty breath of the ocean, churning and breathing, in waves jumping higher than our heads sometimes, in tears, the towels wet in the back of the car after and everywhere you looked, just sand, sand, sand. We counted the beaches at the end of the island summer—was it seventeen, or eighteen?

On each beach, we were reborn.

If we didn't live somewhere in the future, we lived somewhere in the now. We were breaking tenses, breaking rules. We were slowly gathering our courage, through the noise, through the voices, through the dark.

Later, when the kids asked us how we fell in love, we could honestly say, in our bathing suits, under a double rainbow.

i am never ending
i am radiant white light

the tarot of new beginnings

celtic cross spread, present position of the questioner
i turn and it's the sun
my eyes tear up, can it be true

immediate influence and destiny cards
princess of cups and princess of coins
a new way to walk in the world
with a slowly maturing depth of emotion
and the promise of a future

the distant past, the ten of wands
the burden of hard work, responsibility
something weighing on you completed

recent past, the princess of wands
earthy part of fire, reinvigorated by curiosity, enthusiasm
readiness to embark on a new adventure

for the future, the five of coins
still struggle ahead, but maybe now you will be ready

the questioner position, the tower
the need to let go of old patterns, chaos and upheaval and
radical transformation
environmental factors, the seven of swords reversed
a turning in your luck, confession or a truth revealed

inner emotions, the eight of coins
a time to dedicate yourself to your work, the breath of concentration

final result, the emperor
a hope for a future with leadership, power, and authority

i
am
the
sun

i
am
radiant.
white.
light.

afterword

ON NOVEMBER 27TH, 2024, I stood at a podium as the guest speaker at UPEI's MacLauchlan Awards for Effective Writing. I spoke about stories, and about fear. About what it means to write when you're uncertain, or grieving, or unsure whether your voice belongs at all. Some of those words have stayed with me. I offer them again here, at the end of this collection, not as instruction, but as a gentle spark—one that might help ignite your own. Because writing, like grief, doesn't follow a tidy arc. It moves in spirals. It rises and recedes. And still, we write. Not because we've mastered it, but because the stories inside us refuse to stay quiet.

My first book, a travel memoir, began with stillness and loss. A story about miscarriage, about a mother and father trying to remember how to laugh. Editors had said it was unmarketable. But I stood at a public mic at a "Pitch the Publisher" contest, heart pounding, and told the truth I had. Not the grand version—the human one. I talked about how I wanted to go to Thailand, and sit in the heat, and forget. To wait for the emptiness. And I talked about two people who had to teach each other how to live again, and to fill their lives with laughter and joy amidst the grief. I talked about sitting in the heat of Thailand, waiting for the emptiness. It was vulnerable. It was enough.

This is the way of story. It's not about perfect sentences or clever adjectives. It's not found in the forests of punctuation. It's about relationship—to the land, to each other, to the unspoken parts of ourselves. Story carries our joy and our sorrow. It simmers. It burns. It teaches. Because writing—real writing—isn't about polish or perfection. It lives in the story. In the transformation. In the contract between writer and reader, between the self and the world. I didn't start writing because I was fearless. I wrote in fear. I wrote while grieving. I wrote because there was something inside me that would not let go.

Writing is a long apprenticeship in listening. Your stories know you better than you know yourself. They do your emotional labour. They track your transformations. And over time, if you return to them with care, they will begin to speak with clarity and resonance. You will find your authorial voice not through force, but through presence.

If you are wondering whether your story is enough—let me tell you, it is. Your stories are already speaking to you. They simmer quietly in the background. They hold your sorrow, your joy, your changes. They know you better than you think. And one day, if you sit still long enough, they will start to rise. They will begin to burn.

And it doesn't have to happen every day. It can happen on the kitchen floor. In an airport lounge. On a receipt. When you're ready, it will come. The point is not speed. The point is showing up, again and again, even when the stories feel far away. We walk through fire. We swim up from the sea. We write in the dark. We doubt. We begin again. There are a few things I've learned along the way. First, take risks. Write the books you want to see in the world. Don't limit yourself by genre. Let poetry bleed into memoir, essay into fiction. Write what's true—whatever shape it takes.

Second, when things slow down, build structure. I kept a wildly chaotic spreadsheet called "Submission Friday" for ten years, where I tracked every rejection, every maybe, every small win. That little table of colour-coded persistence became a quiet record of belief.

Third, get help. Find your people. Editors, mentors, writer-friends. Ask them to read your first chapters. Talk through structure, share timelines, vent about doubt. At Pownal Street Press, we call it the Editor's Mind Meld. It's the connective tissue of the writing life—community, conversation, vision.

Eventually, the writing will speak for itself. A career is built one story at a time. And when it falters—because it will—when the baby is crying, or the dog needs walking, or the new job swallows your hours, remember this: you are still a writer. You are always a writer. Even when you forget.

When your own stories begin to bore you, read the stories of others. Let them pull you back into possibility. Remember the lineage you belong to—of thinkers and feelers, philosophers and poets, all of them trying to find language for what it means to be here.

At Pownal Street Press, we obsess about story. Every day, we speak with writers who believe their stories can change the world. And we believe them. Not because the stories are always polished, but because they are real. And real stories—when told with courage—become light. I still have my own doubts. The stories keep me up. But it's storytellers who keep me going.

This collection is a letting-go. A flare. A quiet offering to anyone who wonders if their voice belongs. I hope you find yourself somewhere in it. And if you're not quite ready to write—wait. The words will come. And when they do, let them burn bright.

Your story matters. Let it live. If you feel called to write, follow it. Not because it's easy. But because it's yours. Because somewhere out there, someone is waiting for your story to help them find their own.

about the author

MO DUFFY is a writer and editor devoted to the art and architecture of storytelling. Her creative life began at a public microphone, pitching an "unmarketable" travel memoir about grief and healing after still-birth—a book that became her debut, *Unpacked*, published in 2017.

Mo holds an MFA in Creative Nonfiction from Vermont College of Fine Arts, where she studied under some of North America's literary greats. She revised chapters while nine months pregnant, wrote essays between diaper changes, and learned to trust the pulse of her own authorial voice.

In the years that followed, Mo deepened her love of literary culture by launching *Cargo Literary*, a digital magazine devoted to narrative across borders. With three friends and a call for submissions, they published five years' worth of essays, poetry, and visual art until the babies outnumbered the editors.

She has written for literary journals, culture publications, and hybrid digital spaces, and worked with writers as a book coach through her editorial company, *Plotline Book Coaching*. In 2020, she co-founded

Pownal Street Press, a boutique hybrid publishing house grounded in story-first publishing and author-centered care.

Mo is the former executive director of the PEI Writers' Guild and has spoken widely about the writing life—from literary festivals to university classrooms, where she reminds young writers that *even the messy drafts matter.*

She is drawn to the power of story in all forms, from essays and memoirs to children's books written in the early hours of sleepless nights—including one of her own unpublished storylines, about a barn owl named Vera who just wants to dance.

Mo lives in Charlottetown, Prince Edward Island, where she continues to write, publish, parent, and guide others toward the brave, luminous work of telling their truths.

acknowledgements

FOR MY TIRELESS QUEENS Laura, Genevieve, Margaret Ann, and Steph, for bringing me into your homes, with your families, for Canada Days, Thanksgivings, and Christmases, for all of the firsts that I couldn't have endured without you, bathed in the constant love of friendship and trust.

For Kerry Loughlin, who showed me what *framily* can be, and whom I will always consider a guardian of this passage from one universe to another, a burst of Sagittarian light in the darkness.

For my family, for their protection and always being on the end of a hug or a phone call, through disorientation, when I was out to sea, wandering out there in the greens and blues of the ocean, tangled in fishermen's nets and adrift, and for helping me know that you can always come home.

For my littles, Vades and Goose, for giving me the presence of popcorn and movie nights, bike rides to the end of the earth, dog walks and music and for forever teaching me to stop for beauty, devour longevity, and for the constant reminders that grief is a feeling to show and tell, not to push away.

For Lei, my best friend and sounding board, for letting me be a wild teenager again while I figured all of this out, for mac and cheese at midnight, for letting me grow in a sometimes uncertain world, for scream-singing Taylor Swift over pancakes with littles, and for the beautiful guidance and mothering love you have shown them through all of this.

For Mitch, for allowing me to breathe consciousness into these pages, and for never once making me feel like I was moving on alone, for being brave and being better and for doing it our own way, and for Joe, for keeping his heart.

For my first readers and editors, Genevieve Loughlin and Danielle Loewen, for their continuous support through the writing process, and for everyone who has worked with care and love on this title, Alison and Jordan and Ash.

For Dylan Blane, for your love every day, for being here, and for showing me that somehow past these pages, there is a future.